A *Writer's* Roadmap

Also by this author

Fiction

Sunsets of Tulum

Celadon

Nonfiction

*In the Sunlight of Sakurajima:
My Two Years Living in
Southern Japan*

*Cape Cod, Martha's Vineyard,
& Nantucket*

Ray Bartlett has also co-authored over three dozen travel guides for Lonely Planet and other top industry publishers, many of them New York Times and Amazon best sellers. He has written about the United States, Canada, Japan, Korea, Mexico, Tanzania, East Africa, Guatemala, Indonesia, Central America, and other places around the globe.

A Writer's Roadmap

Make your writing dreams come true.

By

Ray Bartlett

Kaisora Press
Cape Cod, USA

Copyright © 2020 by Ray Bartlett

All rights reserved. No part of this publication may be reproduced, stored or transmitted in any form or by any means, electronic, mechanical, photocopying, recording, scanning, or otherwise without written permission from the publisher. It is illegal to copy this book, post it to a website, or distribute it by any other means without permission.

First edition

ISBN: 978-1-7348473-1-4

Library of Congress Control Number: 2020906383

Cover art by Marina Katayeva

Printed in the United States of America

For my dad, with love.

And for everyone who has ever dreamed of being a writer, no matter where you are in the process and whatever your goals may be.

Acknowledgments

Many people helped inform this book, but none more than my dad, whose tireless efforts to write his own novel (and my discussions with him about how to do that) formed so much of this book – a book I wish I'd had ready before he started so that he could have used it all along.

I would like to give particular thanks to Marina Katayeva for such a wonderful cover image, and to readers and editors Danniel P., Nancy B., Andri T., Devon Ellington, Julie Lipkin, Al Waitt, and many others. Thanks also to my family and friends. You all provided excellent feedback and comments as I strove to offer a book that would meet a variety of diverse writerly needs.

Table of Contents

Acknowledgments

Introduction

1. The Vital Importance of Craft
2. Getting Started
3. Magical Mentors
4. Goal-Setting for Clarity and Success
5. Making Luck Happen
6. Queries and Agents and Publishers, Oh My!
7. Persist or Perish
8. When Writer's Block Rears its Ugly Head
9. Re-evaluate
10. Managing Success

About the Author

Also by Ray Bartlett

Introduction

This book is for everyone who has ever wanted to be a writer but felt like there's no roadmap for them to follow. Information is everywhere, but it's hard to find a sense of direction. You know where you are, but how can you get to that far-off place you want to be? You have the big picture in your mind, you have inspirations and energy, but when it comes to actually making all that happen, to knowing what you need to do, or do next, or where you should start, or where you should go … you're lost.

Because you have no roadmap.

Until now.

If you want to be a doctor, or a lawyer, or a civil engineer, or a teacher, or nearly any other profession, there's a roadmap already there for you. You have steps: exams to take, degrees to earn, residencies or internships, and voilá, you're there. Luck plays a part, but you can plot a chart of what you need to accomplish between where you are today and where you want to be. You can go into a guidance counselor's office and say, "I want to be a lawyer" and be presented with a chart that shows all the boxes you need to tick to get there.

If you say you want to be a writer they'll nod, shrug, and say "Your guess is as good as mine."

You're on your own.

And, unfortunately, what works for one person may not work for you. The stroke of luck or genius that someone had was theirs, not yours. The agent who signed your friend or peer or colleague may not have any interest in signing you. Your work may not suit them or perhaps it's just not good enough yet. Or they're busy. Who knows.

It's easy to feel overwhelmed by the difficulty of pursuing your writing dreams, whether it's to write that novel you always wanted or to turn writing into your full-time career.

This book is what I wish I'd had when I was a fledgling writer trying to start my career, and it's based on what I've been teaching at writing groups from California to Boston and beyond.

It will coax you through *creating your own individual roadmap* so that you know exactly where your next steps are. And don't worry: It's not generic advice. This will work for *you*, specifically, because by the end of this read you'll have a process in mind, a way to create and keep creating, a way to choose wisely, and a sense of direction that will apply to your own individual needs, no matter where you are in the writing process and no matter what your goals may be.

As hard as all of this is, there's no magic to it. You just need to know how to make your own roadmap. It's simple: Plot a destination, figure out where the pit stops are, and then start driving. It may take a while, but you'll get there.

It worked for me. It will work for you too.

A *Writer's* Roadmap

A *Writer's* Roadmap

1

The Vital Importance of Craft

There are no shortcuts here. If you want to become a writer you have to learn to write. Not just to write, but to write *well*. You have to become a master of the craft. And nothing, nothing, will change that.

Again: *To become a writer, you have to learn to write.*

Let me stop right here and say that if you plan to debate me on this, you can put the book down right now. What I have to say won't be useful if you are one of those "writers" who think they're going to rocket to the top thinking it's artsy to not know when to use a semicolon or tell the difference between "their" and "there." Not that we can't all make mistakes now and then, a goof or a slip, but really, to want to be a writer and not think the craft matters is like wanting to be a baseball star but not wanting to learn to use a bat.

Assuming we're all on the same page about the importance of craft, let's go over the ways that you can make your craft better.

And realize that this will be a harder road for some of you than others. Writing well is both a craft and an art. We'll touch more on that in this chapter, but keep in mind that both take hard work, dedication and practice. It doesn't happen overnight. And it's not easy.

Some of us are lucky enough to have been born to write. Not that we were born writing. In fact, writing – unlike art, unlike music, unlike mathematics, unlike science –

has no prodigies. No four-year-old savant has ever written a manuscript that is worthy of a bookstore shelf. Issac Asimov's first short story, "Marooned off Vesta," was published when he was eighteen. Many writers reach their groove much later than that, in their forties and fifties or sixties. Henry Miller was forty-three when *Tropic of Cancer* was first published. Many find that their best work comes much later in their career. You just have to live life for a while and understand the depths of the human experience before you can produce work that's going to be widely compelling.

But the drive to write, the urge, the need – *that* can be something one is born with. And some people just have a knack for writing from the start. They're naturals. It'll be easier for them, just like a savant with a piano or a basketball player who is naturally tall.

Despite that, you can still become a writer even if you weren't born with a pen in your hand. Just prepare to work at it a little more.

Train yourself to write the way a marathon runner trains to run.

Put in a word, this is "Quantity."

Don't worry about the quality, not yet, but write, write, *write*. Get in the habit of putting words down, even if you'll never read them again. Condition your body and mind to write. You have to build up this mental and physical stamina just the way an athlete would.

"Um," I hear you saying. "An athlete? Aren't you just sitting on your butt all day?"

Yes, that's *exactly* it. Just like a marathon runner, you need to condition yourself so that an hour or more at a keyboard a day becomes easy.

There are all kinds of ways to start making writing a part of your daily routine. Chip away at a short story. Write an article. Present a theory or argument. Work on a novel. But make it happen daily.

I kept a near-daily journal from age ten well into college. No matter what else was going on, no matter how tired I became, I would manage to write a few sentences or a paragraph or a page each day before turning off the lights. I tell this story and people interrupt by saying, "So you were already writing great things even in your teens?!" and the answer is a resounding "no." Of course not. Those journals were puerile, angst-filled crap.

I think, somewhere in my cellar, I probably still have piles and piles of those spiral notebooks. Not once have I gone back to them. I don't remember most of what I wrote, but it would embarrass me if I did reread them. I was a lonely teen guy drooling over girls in my class, ogling physical attributes, fantasizing. Thank god I grew up, realized what really matters in relationships, in friendships, in life – those things are what enrich good fiction, what make it useful to readers. Nobody wants to read some teen boy's descriptions of a female classmate's incredible anatomy.

I should burn those journals, as nothing contained in them will ever matter in my writing career. But what was vital about them was the process I developed by writing in them. Through those journals I got used to writing a little bit each day. That was absolutely crucial.

Whether you crumple it up, press "Delete," or save your work for later, it all adds up over time. Because, again, to be a writer, you have to *write*.

Just as I did, you need to train yourself, somehow, be it with a journal or writing exercises or some brainstorming, to get used to writing. Ideally, you want to find that you default to writing. In my case, now I come home from errands or a travel gig or walking the dog and what do I want to do more than anything? Sit at the computer… and write. It's that simple. No matter what else is going on during the day, I'm at a point in my life where it's easy, where it's natural, where it's necessary…to sit at the computer and write. It's just my default place to be. You need it to be yours, too.

You'd be surprised how many people seem to think that being a writer comes somehow by *not* writing. People will come up to me and express interest in being a writer, or say, "You have the coolest job; I could do that!" and I ask them how much writing they do.

And they laugh and shake their head. "None," is the answer. "I don't."

I have often given people this little piece of advice: *"There is no one thing you can do to guarantee you'll become a writer; however, there are many things you can do to guarantee you won't become one."*

Not writing is up at the top of the list. You will never be a writer if you don't train yourself to write. For now, *just as I did with my journal in grade school*, don't worry about what you're writing. Don't worry if it's good or bad. Don't worry about showing anyone.

Just write. Get yourself into the habit of writing. *Writing daily.*

Train yourself, so that today you're doing fifteen minutes of writing. Tomorrow do twenty. In a year, you're doing an hour of writing a day. If you can write an hour a day, even if that's all you do that day, you'll easily be able to produce enough work to be a writer.

Some people find it easier to write in terms of pages or by word count. Whatever your method, the key thing is to start making some writing happen daily.

I can't stress that enough. It's rock simple, but it's at the heart of everything that will come later as you reach your writing goals: You *have* to be able to write for hours and hours, like that marathon runner.

Additionally, you have to write well.

So if that first part was "Quantity," now we'll talk "Quality." Because you also won't be a writer (or you won't be an author) if, at some level, what you write isn't good.

"Good writing" is a vague, often misunderstood word, but allow me to define it as work that other people enjoy reading. Writing is a strange thing, because initially, for nearly all of us, writing is more narcissistic than anything else. We write because of our own need to process our thoughts, feelings, and emotions, and for many of us, the audience remains essentially ourselves. We laugh at our own hilarity, admire our own brilliance, grin as our razor-sharp repartee cuts real and imagined foes to the bone.

But at a certain point, our writing has to venture off into the real world, a world of readers far more discerning and far less enthusiastic than ourselves. Like a salmon egg hatching in fresh water and growing for a while, at some point, our writing has to go off into the deep blue sea. A metamorphosis happens. The focus turns away from ourselves and to others. And at this point, your writing really needs to be good if you want to pursue writing as a career.

Let me also define "good writing" as work that ideally means writing that people *outside your circle of friends and family* will enjoy reading. Your eventual audience. The deep blue sea.

Not that there's anything wrong with writing for yourself, or just for family, or just for friends. Many people do just that. If that's your end goal, then the path will be slightly easier for you. Friends and family are far more willing to give you the benefit of the doubt, too. They're predisposed to like your work, and they want to support and encourage you.

For most of us looking to a wider audience, wanting to be professional writers and even earning a living at it, there's a battle that has to occur: We have to hook a reader. Most people come to a book apprehensive. They don't automatically like a work just because it's there. They may have come to love a certain author and hunger for anything new that person has produced. But for the unknown writer (i.e. you!), it's a challenge to gain readers. And for a while, anyway, you'll be the unknown writer.

So your writing *really has to be good.*

It has to be better than good.

It has to be really, *really* good.

I would argue that even if you're writing for your friends and family, you still need to offer the very best work you can possibly can...or you're wasting a reader's time. And your own.

This is why honing your craft is so important, and why – for most of us – it takes a lot of time. Years or even decades. If you've always hated grammar, don't feel you're alone (hardly anyone is born loving grammar!) but you won't escape having to become an expert in it. Each comma, period, and mark of punctuation is vital to a reader's interaction with your ideas. Careful, consistent grammar and spelling instantly work to establish you as an expert, and for many readers your flawless prose will be their very first impression of your work. If readers spot errors or see shoddy craft, they may not stick around long enough to appreciate your great ideas. Professionals certainly won't. They've got a hundred perfect pages to choose from. Not choosing yours because you're still learning the craft makes it easy to send your submission into the trash.

Luckily for us, developing yourself as a writer is easier now than it's ever been. This topic is what nearly all the existing resources focus on, from instruction books to writing classes that now, incredibly, are as effective online as they are in real, face-to-face ones. There's a wealth of very well-written books to help you through this, but there's a catch too: The best books in the world won't help you if you never actually write (remember, that's why I started with "Quantity").

They also won't help you if you're one of those who thinks you're the next Steinbeck and don't need to improve your craft. Oddly, there's an inverse curve: The better people believe their writing to be, the worse it usually is.

So take the courses, read the books, do whatever is necessary to bring your writing up to the level of the professional.

Many, if not most, resources on improving your writing focus only on this one issue – craft - and I am not going to rehash that here. This is a roadmap, not a creative writing course. It's simple, clear, straightforward advice on how to reach your writing dreams. I'll list some ways to improve your craft; however, it's up to you to charge ahead and improve it.

Self-study

Get books on writing out of the library or from a bookstore. Read them, do the exercises. Internalize the lessons. From grammar to art. (This is by no means a complete list: *On Writing Well* by William Zinsser, *Bird by Bird* by Anne Lamott, *The Art of Fiction* by John Gardner, *The Elements of Style* by Strunk & White, *Writing Fiction* by Janet Burroway, *On Writing* by Stephen King, *A Poetry Handbook* by Mary Oliver, and many more.) There are lots of them, and new ones will come out to supplement these classics.

Read them all. Grok as many as you can. Use what's useful; discard what's not. Strunk & White's *Elements of Style* is considered near holy. Get in the habit of using a dictionary rather than your spell-checker – sometimes spelling isn't the problem, but the nuances in your usage of the word.

Read, read, read

Don't just read books on good writing, read good books. Great literature will inspire you, impress you, and you'll develop a sense of story arc and drama at the same time. You'll internalize, even if you can't explain or define it, good storytelling. If you're writing fiction, read fiction. If you're writing mysteries, read mysteries. Become an expert in your chosen spot on the bookshelf. Read as often and as much as you can.

Join writing groups

Many people want to join a writing group, a bunch of similarly minded folks who can assist you in improving your writing. Often this is an easy entry into the world of being critiqued and can be a good way to get feedback about your writing. You take turns distributing work in progress (or final drafts, whatever you want to share) and each person will read it over the break, and then bring their feedback for you in the next class. You'll get a sense of how your work resonates with some test readers, and it is useful to get criticism and feedback.

Writing groups can be a useful stepping-stone in the process, but at a certain point they can also act like the isles of the Sirens, where the beautiful singing lured the unsuspecting to their death. One can very easily see the group's views (or a dominant member's view) as the only important view. If a group loves your writing, you may feel as if it's ready for publication when it's completely not.

Conversely, one may end up dejected and depressed because a writing group doesn't get your work, doesn't like or understand it…and stop writing, when the manuscript is actually innovating and lovely. So if you choose to join a writing group, keep some emotional distance, with both the praise and the criticism.

Take online courses

It has gotten easier and easier to make online writing courses work wonders for improving your writing. Nonprofits like Grub Street (www.grubstreet.org) and many colleges and universities offer excellent instruction online. If you can, take these courses. Learn from them. It's one of your best options for professional writing.

If you're in high school, you're getting some of the best instruction for free: It's called English class. Paying attention here will pay off in spades down the road.

Consider MFA programs

Going a step further, there are MFA programs. While these have come under scrutiny in recent years for their high cost, you will likely find the highest possible caliber of instruction here. Your professors will be longtime, respected authors and writers, and your peers will be dedicated, serious writers themselves. MFA programs can provide references for other writing-related jobs, and some are steppingstones to higher-level academic work, such as getting a doctorate in English. Given the cost, you'll need to make your own decision on whether it makes sense. Genre fiction writers may be better off diving into the world of agents and publishers directly, but for literary fiction and short-story writers, especially those who wish to pursue teaching at the university level, an MFA will be worth considering. Alternatively, an MA or PhD may make sense.

Become your own worst critic

A huge problem with beginning writers is that they just aren't hard enough on themselves. It's very easy to think your work is brilliant when it's not. Even if you've got talent, spark, a great idea, and so on, that doesn't mean you'll automatically get it right the first time. Or the second. Or the third. Part of learning to write is learning to spot your own mistakes, discern where you've failed, where your writing is weakest. All without losing faith in yourself and your project overall. It's a complex balancing act, but it's vital to becoming a professional writer.

Develop a thick skin

Another easy mistake to make is to take someone's feedback too personally, or worse, to get offended and huffy. Unless someone's actually trying to hurt or undermine you (in which case, why show them your work at all?), they're offering you a chance to see what someone outside your own skin will see when they pick up your work. It's extremely valuable to have others' opinions, and paradoxically, it's far more vital to have people point out the shortcomings than give out praise. If you're doing something well, great, you nailed it. But seeing, addressing, and fixing the flaws is what will really get your manuscript ready for showing to the world. Keep yourself aware that someone's not criticizing you or your effort, but trying to make the project better.

Being able to take criticism well serves another purpose down the road: Should you make it, should you get it out into the real world, books will be attacked by critics and readers from all walks of life, and if you can't shrug off someone's comment you'll end up paralyzed. You can probably list a few books you thought were awful, not worthy of being published, some that you just couldn't wait to put down. People will feel like that about your book too sometimes. It's part of the process, and that's totally fine.

No matter what, your first responsibility as a serious writer is to increase both the quantity and quality of what you produce. Once you reach a certain proficiency, you're ready to get started going somewhere.

2

Getting Started: Interest and Momentum

So we've talked about some key elements that you'll need to work on with your writing, but say you've gotten to a certain level of confidence, you feel your writing is solid, and you're still working at a fast-food joint or for a 9-to-5 you hate and are ready for a change.

How do you get started?

Two concepts here to think about: interest and momentum.

Think like a bank: generate interest

Think about your writing as you would think about a savings account: You want it to be generating interest. (Note, haha, the pun, which, yes, I do intend.) You want it to be interesting for your readers, but you also want to have a *return on your investment.*

By that I mean that each time you sit down to write or you send your work off somewhere or you publish an article, you want that to be moving you somewhere in your career – generating "interest" the way money accrues in the bank. If you've written an article for your college newspaper, that's not just an article that vanishes and fades as soon as the next issue comes out. You've always got that in your "bank." When you're writing a query, you can refer to that (within reason) as something you've written that helps establish you as a writing professional.

So especially as you're starting out, don't discount the small stuff. In fact, that is how most writers ascend the ladder of their writing career. Even if something you write gets rejected, you've gotten further along, you're more experienced, and you may have learned from your mistakes along the way.

People have a tendency, especially as beginners, to think that certain work is beneath them. They may not want to "waste time" submitting to a local newspaper because they think their work is only worth of *The New York Times*. Or the other way around: Their work isn't even worthy of a small newspaper because they're just a beginner.

In reality, it's those smaller places that will lead you to bigger places, and those bigger places will eventually make your writing garner the attention. There's really little difference between writing and baseball: Someone who has spent years on the field and in the dugout, who has studied games and played countless hours, even if some of that was in a backyard or at the company barbecue – they'll be far more professional than someone who's barely swung a bat before. So think of this as the backyard barbecue baseball game where someone's calling, "Hey, can anyone take left field?"

So get out there and write.

As a beginner, here are some places you can try to get a toe in the door:

1. Local newspapers used to be a standby, but as journalism has hit hard times, the local newspaper may be long gone, or if it's still there, it may be struggling. But you may be the reporter they're looking for. Or query them for a column. Write opinion pieces. Even if it's a letter to the editor, you can still say your "work has appeared in the XYZ Times." (This can haunt you later if you try to pass it off as more than that. People do check details, so you want to be factual.)

2. If you're a fiction writer or poet, see what writing groups are nearby by visiting the local library. Sign up. Start immersing yourself in writing and writers.

3. Prizes and contests offer a way to make your work stand out, though there's a caveat emptor here. Buyer beware. Some

contests masquerade as such but really just pull in big bucks for the organizers with little or no benefit going to the entrants or winners.

4. *Poets & Writers* magazine is a nearly holy magazine for writers of all stripes, with very good info on opportunities, contests, prizes, and the like.

5. Find writing opportunities online. These don't have to be local, and even beginning writers can do work on contract. It's tough to list these in a print book, as they are ever-changing, but even places like online classified ads often have sections where artists or writers are needed for small jobs.

6. Go to your local newsstand or bookstore and find the magazine section. Pick out magazines you've read yourself, and try to find an article you think you could use as a template and then write (or at least query) about that to the magazine.

For example, you like pottery and noticed a recent article in a local magazine about glassblowers. Query the magazine's editor (always check if they have submissions guidelines first!) by finding their name in the masthead (the page toward the beginning with all the editors' names). Then see if they might want a similar article but on pottery. Lots of times editors are willing to take a chance if you've given them a good idea.

7. If you're a college student, there are lots of university opportunities you can take advantage of. College newspapers and literary magazines, contests, intercollegiate prizes, and so on. Get familiar with what is out there and then dive into being a part of it.

8. If you're having difficulty identifying places, you can try asking your kindly and always-knowledgeable librarian to help you sleuth down some books or opportunities. (Though, remember, nobody other than you is going to make you a writer! You're the one who needs to propel this forward.)

Each little place you manage to publish in or create for, you're generating interest, and over time, these little blips and blurbles become something bigger, just the way saving a penny here and there in a bank leads to mucho money down the road. Suddenly, you can say something like, "I've been writing professionally for seven years" or "My work has been featured in dozens of magazines." You're dropping a quarter here, a nickel there, a dollar … and over time, it's a nest egg of size.

Momentum: It's a good thing.

You know that image of a rock at the top of a hill, balanced precariously but not moving anywhere?

That's you starting out.

You've got all these great ideas, a lot of energy, and you're dying to "be a writer" in however you define it to be. You just aren't going anywhere.

What you need is to get that rock moving.

So find ways to push and get it inching, then finally rolling down the hill – because once it's got momentum it won't want to stop. Once that writing "rock" is finally rolling, it will keep rolling unless you do things to slow it down.

I remember as a high school student thinking "A ten-page paper? Is that teacher insane?!" and then in college it was "A fifty-page paper? What?!" and then I felt like a superhero when I completed my first novel manuscript that topped out at about two hundred pages. Now whipping out 3000 words a day feels "easy," and I don't even bat an eyelash about knocking out a three-hundred-page novel. I'm used to it. I've got a whole bookshelf full of books I've worked on, written, co-authored. Something like three dozen country guides. As many or more other one-off titles. I've written for names most people recognize, like *USA Today* and *Lonely Planet*. When I query, I've got a list of highly respectable places to include that establish me as a damn good writer to anyone in the field.

But it wasn't always like that.

Just like you, I started out as a rock on the top of a hill, got it rolling very slowly by writing in small publications, and then kept plugging away at it until I got where I am today. As I've mentioned, there are exceptions, writers who seem to just plop into a magical good thing and stay there. But most of us work hard, keep at it, and eventually see our careers take shape over time.

Should I work for free?

This is a tricky one, because everyone feels different about this and working for free can sometimes be a way to get that giant rock rolling. You certainly can. You'll have plenty of opportunities to put your time and energy into someone else's project … and not get a cent from it.

But I recommend against it.

Why?

Because at some level, unless you're independently wealthy and truly don't care about earning a living with this crazy writing thing, you will want to be paid. You've put your intellect, your time, and your skill into something that darn well has value (to whoever is using it, publishing it, etc.). Would you expect a doctor to give you free checkups or a painter to come over and do your house for free? No way.

Yet time and time again, writers, photographers, and artists are asked (or sometimes expected) to give away their work for free.

I was fine, in college, to accept that I wasn't going to be paid for work I submitted to the college newspaper or literary magazine. But in college, I started to submit to local newspapers (I had editorial cartoons, a comic strip, and articles), and I just told myself that I would not work for free. If I wanted to be a writer, to earn a living off it, I needed to make sure there was some kind of legitimate compensation.

That's not to say I don't happily volunteer my time or writing for causes or for people I believe in. That's a different thing. You can give generously of your time and skills to help make the world a better place and to support the people you love and care about.

As mentioned above, there are places (such as small lit mags) where payment is not possible, or where remuneration is only in copies of the magazine. Nothing wrong with that. You're still generating momentum for your career (and thus a value) by their publishing your work.

But if you're being hired, if someone's making money off of the work you're creating, you should be paid. Freelance writers have every right to not begin a work until a contract has been signed. And you should be getting a byline, too, unless it's entirely work for hire, such as copywriting for a corporation.

I have been lucky enough to have most of my contracts work out just fine, and only a few times has it been necessary to go into the fine print. However, one project had every indication of going forward, the editor was super-nice, I had booked my tickets and made hotel reservations ... and then the publisher pulled the plug. Luckily for me, I'd signed a contract and they were legally bound to honor it. So I got paid even though I never wrote the book ... the easiest gig I've ever had. Most entail grueling amounts of work, and the pay (if you calculate it hourly) is about USD$3.80/hour. I love what I do. I'm doing what I love. But I didn't feel too bad for holding them to that contract when the book was canceled. Most of the time I think publishers are getting a very reasonable deal.

On the flip side, free work can give you bylines that may actually help you get that rock rolling, so there can be a time and a place when that makes sense. If you find yourself in a position where you're always working for free, where you're never able to interest someone in hiring you directly, then you may want to re-evaluate whether this strategy is getting you anywhere.

To help answer that, and many other "Am I good enough?" questions, you'll need to find a mentor.

3

Magical Mentors

Mentors are professionals in the field who are willing to assist you with your writing. They can come from all walks of life and do not necessarily have to be professional writers themselves, though you'll find that as you improve your own craft, having trusted professional advice becomes increasingly more valuable. But mentors will read, evaluate, comment, criticize, and praise your work, giving you a sense of not just what your accomplishments are, but what steps you need to take next. They are like unicorns: magical and sprinkled with fairy dust and glitter.

Finding a good mentor will be the next break in your writing career.

The value of mentors

Let's face it, writing is a strange gig, partly because (for the beginner) it seems so arbitrary. We've all heard stories about how some best seller got rejected by fifty publishers before rocketing to the top of The New York Times Best Seller list and staying there for three thousand weeks. We've heard of people writing two pages in a query letter and getting six-figure advances. We've heard of people working for decades only to finally be "discovered," and being set for the rest of their lives.

Many of these stories, if not most, are urban legends. Fake news. But a few are true.

This will not happen to you. (Okay, to most of you.)

Most of you – nearly all – will find success as a writer by carefully and diligently following a path you find works for you.

Your roadmap. It will probably take longer than you think, and it may be harder than you think. But if you stick to it, and persist, you will see that you're making progress.

Mentors are vital to this progress, because they're the people who not only "get" you, your ideas, your dreams, but who also see what's holding you back as well. They're the ones who will offer you real constructive criticism (emphasis on the criticism) so that you will push yourself, improve, and get to the next level. They'll have a sense of craft, of quality, of arc; they'll see the work as it is and how you intend it to be.

And trust me on this: Mentors are golden. Treat them as precious, because they are.

How and where to find mentors

If you are lucky, you'll find mentors among your family or friends. Someone who really knows writing, someone who reads widely, someone who loves exactly the kind of writing you're planning to do. Your first mentor might be also be a teacher, either in school, at university, or from a workshop you took.

But you may need to find them elsewhere, too. Even peers who understand your work can even be mentors, especially if they're ahead of you in their writing careers. At some point, you'll want to consider getting professional mentoring that you'll pay for.

Evaluating a mentor

The best way to tell if someone isn't a good mentor is to see how adoring they are of your writing. If all they can say is "Five stars," "I loved it," "This is great," without also going into concrete ways you can improve, then you should instantly back away and find another mentor. That is opposite to the affirmation that many beginners want, but you are in this game to improve … not to pat yourself on the back all the time.

A constructively critical mentor will help you to identify your shortcomings, allowing you to improve. You won't get anywhere as a writer if people just tell you that they "loved it." It's flattering, sure. It makes you feel good, but it's useless for your growth as a writer. To grow, you need to identify and fix the problems. (If you want affirmation, read your novel to your dog. They'll love you and won't find a single thing wrong with the manuscript.)

So find mentors who will offer you useful, even harsh, criticism. Be prepared for a lot of criticism. Ultimately, your work will have to pass a gantlet of critics on its way to the bookshelf: someone reading the slushpile at the agent's office, the agent himself/herself, an editor or two or ten, a publishing team. If your writing can't stand up to those people's criticism, it won't stand up at all.

When to hire a mentor

Mentors can be free or paid, and you may find that paying someone – an objective third party – is actually a good use of your money and time. Sometimes people will be happy to read your work for free and give just as good a critique. But it is often hugely valuable to get someone professional to spend time with your work, evaluating not only your page-by-page caliber, but offering suggestions and hints on where best to perform triage. Find professional mentors by searching online, finding writing non-profits, checking writing forums, asking at creative writing groups, or contacting university English or extracurricular learning departments for recommendations.

How not to upset your mentor

Mentors, paid or not, are devoting a fair amount of time to your project at the expense of things they'd rather be doing with their time. And nobody will be as enamored with your manuscript as you. So be respectful and appreciative of your mentor's taking the time to read it, even if you're paying them. Be willing to listen to their criticism, maybe even painfully direct words, about a work that you're deeply involved with. Ultimately, they'll dramatically increase your chances of pursuing your writing dream. So be nice.

The quickest way to upset a mentor is to counter everything they're bringing up with the argument "You're just not getting it," or "You're not the right audience." They know the audience better than you do. Listen to them. Hang on every word they say. You can always prove them wrong down the road. But more than likely, they are more in tune with the writing field than you are.

If a reader isn't getting it, guess whose fault that is. Is it the reader's fault? Not at all. It's the writer's fault. The fact you have to even counter with that argument is proof that yes, indeed, you the writer have more work to do. Furthermore, your mentor is already on your side, already predisposed to like your work, and far more willing to see it through to the end than an unknown reader would be.

Many beginning writers fall into an unfortunate "They don't know what they don't know" trap, where it's easy to write off valid, important criticism as wrong or as superfluous because the wannabe writer simply can't see how flawed their own work is. (Remember that daily journal I kept that I never want to read again? At the time, I thought every word I put down there was pure gold.)

So approach any feedback you get with the presupposition that the mentor is right and you're wrong. Nobody will force you to change anything if you happen to be right, but discounting feedback - any feedback - is not going to help you. Be willing to consider that your mentor may be a better judge of your work than you are. If you've chosen them correctly, that's exactly what will happen. And you need their time and expertise to help you improve.

Should you pay your mentor?

In a word: Yes.

A professional opinion in the field is gold, so it's absolutely reasonable for a mentor to charge a fee that makes reading your work worth their time. Agents charge between ten to twenty percent off the income from the sale of your book, but a mentor won't receive anything, even if the book becomes a best seller. If a mentor is offering you valuable help and direction, pay them and be sure to acknowledge your appreciation when the book sells.

Even if it's a friend, a nonprofessional, even if someone doesn't ask to be paid, pay them in-kind somehow. Acknowledgment in the back of the book. A free copy. A nice dinner or drink at their favorite bar. Make them breakfast. But show them, tangibly, that they're appreciated and you value their taking the time to make your book better.

Eventually, you may find that you've outgrown the need for mentors. Or an editor or publisher will serve the mentorship role. But for those of us starting out at the beginning of our careers, a mentor or two will be invaluable.

4

Goal-Setting for Clarity and Success

Now that we've gotten through some basics, such as quantity, quality, and mentorship, it's time to set some goals.

Goals? Why do we need them?

We need to set specific goals because, far too often, people assume that writing, be it writing a novel or making writing a career, will just somehow *happen*. That you walk into it. Or it walks into you.

It doesn't.

You'll become a writer because you set out very carefully to be one. And a key part of that is setting specific goals, then meeting or exceeding them.

These not only give you a sense of direction, they let you see where you've been and how far you've come. All of that helps to push you onward and upward.

Setting goals

Think for a moment of your writing dreams as a staircase. Wherever you are in your career right now, you're at the bottom of a staircase. The steps near your feet are the short-term goals. The steps at eye level are your medium-term goals. At the top of the staircase is your long-term goal. Where you'll eventually be.

You need all of these goals. Could you reach the top of a staircase if the bottom five steps were missing? Could you get to the top if you didn't have the middle steps?

No. You need to have all of these in order for goal-setting to work. And goal-setting is vital, whether you're just trying to get a novel written or you want writing as your long-term career.

Short-term goals

Short-term goals are harder to come up with than you think. Lots of people assume it's short-term as in "within a year." No. Short-term goals are things you can do today (or tomorrow, or this weekend) that will move you toward your other goals down the road. Literally, you want to be able to put down this book and start one of the short-term goals today. They are parts of the writing process. Actions. Activities.

So *"Write fifteen minutes a day"* would be a great short-term goal. But don't just sit there. *Go write!*

"Write a query letter to an agent" would be nice. *Make it happen!*

"Search for agents" would work, though it's a bit vague. Get on the computer...*and search!*

Something like "write a good short story" doesn't help you. Why not? Because it's so vague that there's no immediate call to action other than a general "I need to write." You need these short-term goals to be specific, tangible, concrete calls to action that force you to make good use of those moments, those daily moments, when you tend to check social media or do the dishes or clean house...when you could be actually going somewhere with your writing.

Got it? Great. Now take a moment to write down a few short-term goals. Do it now while this is fresh in your mind.

Let's move on to setting the medium-term goals.

Medium-term goals

This category is for what product you'll have when you've accomplished your short-term goals. Where are you heading when you sit down to write? Most of us (though perhaps not all!) are trying to write a book. (And really, this kind of method works for all creative pursuits, not just writing. Art, music, even building a website…you still need short-, medium-, and long-term goals!) It can be a novel, a memoir, a nonfiction piece. Whatever.

So let's start with that:

"Finish my Great American Novel." Perfect. Excellent medium-term goal.

"Finish my memoir."

"Complete the draft of Harry Hamster Heads to Hollywood."

"Write a good short story," might fit in here, though be careful with vague words like "good." Still, this works not as a short-term goal, but as a medium-term one.

What's great about the medium-term goal-setting is that suddenly you can start to see where you'll be in the nearish future. And by "nearish future," let's say a year or two, maybe five at the most. You don't want your medium-term goals to be so far away that there's no urgency. Because, let's face it, there's no time like the present, and the whole reason you're reading this book is to start getting things done.

It doesn't have to be a piece of writing, either:

"Get into an MFA program."

"Start getting paid for my writing somehow."

"Post to my blog weekly."

Just as you might have a workout plan to get your body in shape, so too can you "work out" with your writing. The short-term goals get you (remember the staircase!) up to the medium-term ones.

Now that we know where you're heading with this particular project (and, thanks to the short-term goals, how to get there), let's start thinking long term.

Long-term goals

This is where you really need to ask yourself where you want to be with your writing in five or even ten years. Or maybe even longer. What is your endgame?

Are you planning to be a writer full time, or are you more just hoping to write a book and be done with it? If the latter, then probably you want to sell that book. Why write it if you're just going to keep it in a drawer somewhere?

So for those of you who aren't thinking of writing as a career, maybe because you've already had a rewarding career and are retired, or maybe because you just don't feel like there's inspiration enough for more than one book, go ahead and make "selling my book" the long-term goal.

For those of you who dream of a life spent at the keyboard, these long-term goals can be almost as challenging as the project you're currently working on.

I'll give you an example from my own life. When I was in college, my long-term goal was to win the Nobel Prize in Literature.

That seems a bit comical now, and (see the Re-evaluate chapter for more!) over time, that has shifted a bit. Not that I wouldn't love to win the Nobel Prize for Literature, but as the decades have rolled by I'm a bit less idealistic and a bit more realistic and happy to settle for less. In a good way. I count myself incredibly lucky to have made writing my career for so long, and if the Nobel Prize doesn't plop into my lap I won't feel I've wasted anything.

But all of that said:

I chose that goal because I've always wanted to write deep, important, life-altering literature. Whether or not my novels ever reach the fame or acclaim necessary to win a Nobel Prize, that's been my guiding light as I write them. I want these works to matter in people's lives. I want the characters to be compelling enough to reshape human views about what's important. I want someone to finish my novels and close the book and reflect deeply on their own life, his or her own choices, the decisions we make, our place in this vast human community.

And that's steered me toward a certain part of the bookshelf: the literary fiction section.

Many of you may have entirely different long-term goals. A mystery writer might one day aspire to be the president of the Mystery Writers of America. A goal might be to have a series of mysteries, one per year. A fantasy or romance writer's goals might be equally prolific. In fact, having a series is a very smart way to lure readers into reading not just one, but many of your works. Maybe you want to be a self-help maven and write the next *Chicken Soup for the Soul*.

All of those are valid long-term goals.

So for this, go deep, go long, go grand. Conjure up your dreams and write them here. Figure out where your heart is. This is why you slog away at the keyboard, why you endlessly write and rewrite. And someday – with luck – this is where you'll nod and think, "You know what? I made it. I got here."

Some examples of long-term goals:

- *Write a successful book series (pick your genre).*

- *Be the head of a renowned MFA program.*

- *Teach creative writing at a university.*

- *Win the Nobel Prize in Literature.*

- *Be able to survive financially on your writing alone.*

- *Be a household name.*

- *See your book be made into a movie.*

But wait, hold on. There's another possibility. Maybe you're not trying to win the Nobel Prize or be a household name, but you've got a book you want to see published. Just a book. That's been your dream. You've had a novel or a memoir or something gestating inside you, but nothing beyond that?

Well, that's your long-term goal. Getting that book published and out into the world.

There's no end to the possibilities here, but the value in going through this process is that you'll suddenly have a route to follow. Back to the roadmap analogy: We're on the East Coast, now we know we're going to take a trip to California. Not Florida, not Maine. Maybe along the way we head to Canada or down into Tennessee, but we know that we'll start off in New York City and somewhere down the road we'll be in San Francisco or LA. We'll need to get gas in towns W, X, Y, and Z, but if we stick to this plan and keep on driving, we'll get there.

But wait, there's more!

Goals don't have to just be those three time frames: today, next year, next decade. You can break this down like one of those fractal paintings, where each tiny little bud is an exact copy of the larger structure. Give yourself short-, medium-, and long-term goals within your short-term goals. Or your medium-term ones. Writing the first draft of your book? Make "complete the first draft" your long-term goal and work backward, creating medium- and short-term goals to propel you forward.

If you do one thing after putting this book down, make those goals. With clear goals set, you will always know where your next step should be, and you will always have direction, and you will always know where to go.

I can't emphasize enough how important it is to set concrete goals for your writing. When people get off track, get stuck, get frustrated, get writer's block, ninety-nine percent of the time it's just because they've gotten away from their goals … or never set any in the first place.

5

Making Luck Happen

We've all heard people from all walks of life talk about their big break. That unknown actor who finally lands a leading role in a blockbuster. The lawyer who wins a landmark case. The obscure writer who finally sells that best seller and launches forever into the limelight.

That doesn't happen automatically. Luck plays a role, but setting yourself up to have luck happen is vital. It's sort of like that quote about the lottery: You can't win if you don't play.

The big A or B decision

Now that you have a list of short-, medium-, and long-term goals, you can apply the "A or B decision" to nearly every single choice life throws your way.

Picking option A is going to bring you closer to these goals.

Choosing option B will move you farther away.

See where I'm going with this?

This isn't rocket science:

Always choose option A

That's how you will move closer to being a writer and achieving your goals. I talk with so many hopeful writers and when we get down to it, they've spent most of their lives choosing option B. They've taken computer programming in college rather than the English major they enjoyed. They've gotten a job in a bank rather than at a newspaper.

They've gotten married, had kids. Nothing against kids, or being married, but that often pulls people away from their writing goals. At the end of the day they have a drink and watch YouTube videos instead of spending fifteen minutes working on their writing. And they've been choosing option B for years … or for decades.

Writing's always been important to them, yet when I coach them to look at their lives and see the decisions they've made, they realize the obvious: Writing's never been important *enough*.

And, really, if something's not important enough…is it important at all?

This can be a hard pill to swallow sometimes. That you think you really want to write and be a writer … but maybe when it comes down to it, you actually don't. And you know what? Nobody's forcing you to do this. I certainly can't guarantee that this writing thing will lead to happiness or financial success or any of that. Some people may be happier watching cat videos with a good cocktail.

But if that's not you, if somewhere inside you really are burning to be a writer, then luckily there's an easy solution to this nasty cat video addiction you've picked up:

Choose option A.

It happens tonight. Stop watching videos and open that list of short-term goals and work toward one of them. Just do it.

Once you're playing the lottery, suddenly you have a chance to win.

I can look back at some key moments in my own life when luck happened, but I made it happen by consistently choosing A instead of B. It wasn't always easy. In fact, it almost never is.

A good example came when I had just been offered the chance to work for Lonely Planet. It had been a grueling admission process (more in the Persist or Perish chapter!), but I'd passed muster and been offered a gig updating their guidebook to Japan.

And suddenly, within the same darn week, a job offer came in from a Boston-based nonprofit that needed website work done. More importantly, it was paying top dollar, a salary with health insurance and other benefits. It was more money than I'd ever been offered in my life. It would have been an excellent job, and everyone there seemed friendly and very enthusiastic about having me join the team.

But it meant I had to choose between these two great opportunities.

It was A or B.

And of course I chose A. One month later I was touring Japan for one of the world's best-loved travel publications. It was a huge break, really, the "big break" I'd dreamed of. But the pay was next to nothing and it meant weeks or months away from my family. It brought its own problems, but it was clearly the option A, the one that brought me closer to my dream.

I made that luck happen. It didn't happen for me. I chose option A.

A or B will not always be the easy choice to make, but you will find if you consistently choose A, you'll be moving yourself ever closer to those long-term goals. If you choose B, you may find yourself consistently getting farther away. It's that simple.

Another lucky break came when I'd decided to apply for a graduate MFA program. I was newly married, struggling at a desk job that was slurping out my soul, and one of the teachers in my writing group encouraged me to apply for an MFA. There are hundreds, but of the ones I could readily go to, I had two options: Boston University or Emerson College.

The BU program was a crazy-intense one-year thing with a huge scholarship and was, at the time, number three in the *U.S. News & World Report* rankings, third to U of Iowa and Johns Hopkins.

Emerson's option was number twenty on the list, a three-year program that would have required me to go part time for five or six years to complete the degree.

I applied to both, and found out months later that I'd been accepted at Emerson and rejected at Boston University.

So I investigated loans, massive loans, that would be needed to foot the bill for a five- or six-year investment. I talked with my boss about leaving early a few days a week to make the commute up to Boston from Cape Cod. I got all the ducks in a row…

… and then, the Friday before the semester was to begin, I got a call from my wife. (I was at a sales conference that weekend.)

"I think you just got accepted into the BU program," she said.

I didn't dare believe it, but when I called them to verify, it turned out, – amazingly – that I had been number thirteen on a list of twelve spots, and someone had just canceled, opening up the slot for me.

That changed my life. Instead of spending five years, I was done the following spring. Instead of investing more than a hundred thousand dollars, I spent less than ten thousand. I came out with a MA in English, not an MFA. And it was a better program too.

"But that was total luck!" you are saying. "There's no 'Option A' in this tale."

Yeah, you're right. It was total luck. Sometimes you do just get lucky. But on the other hand, I could have just kept on plugging away at a day job. It paid well, and even though I hated it … it paid well.

But I didn't. I chose to apply. I might have been rejected at both places. At least I bought that lottery ticket in the first place.

You can too. Always choose Option A.

Avoid creativity drags.

"I shouldn't talk about my writing because I don't want someone else to steal my idea, right?"

No. The chances of anyone "stealing" your idea are minuscule, and people who worry about this are probably paranoid and should be seeking professional therapy.

Don't talk about your writing because doing this saps your own creative energy and hampers your chances of completing that vital first draft.

Pro Tip: Don't talk about your writing before it's written down.

This really separates the people who want to be writers from the people who just want to be perceived as writers. Oddly, for some, it's more vital to be *viewed as a writer* than to actually produce. The latter will blather endlessly about their ideas, about the works they're in the midst of, about this and that… but rarely if ever complete anything. They're often in writing groups or Meetups or other such workshops so they can be validated by other writers and feel part of a writing community. They're always endlessly working on a novel, getting feedback, submitting it, even. But somehow they never seem to go anywhere.

Writing at its core is a solitary pursuit. Writers are not pack oriented. There's no herd to be a part of. In fact, talking about your work in groups too much or reading too many writing books can be as much a form of procrastination as anything else.

Writers who talk about their writing shoot themselves in the foot in two critical ways:

One, if people like your idea, that positive glow makes it harder to complete it. Ironic, isn't it? Yet if someone gushes to you about what a great idea that is, in many ways, they've already given you the reward before you've even done the work. What you want is a reader to gush about a book that's already written. Talking about the idea is just that: talk. There's no work, you haven't gotten anything accomplished – yet you feel as though you have. You've gotten that connection and kinship, and all without even putting the pen to the page.

Consequently, when you do sit down, you're far more likely to get blocked. You have someone's expectations to live up to, and you have less freedom to still be inspired.

Two, if you tell people your idea and they don't like it, again, the negativity makes it harder to complete it. Why work on a project at all if someone's not going to like it anyway? Even though your idea may be great, and maybe just your telling of it (or the other person's perception of it) makes it seem less rosy, you're still fighting an uphill battle against the negativity. When you get blocked, it's that much harder to keep going when you know that your future reader isn't going to like it anyway.

Either way, whether your listeners love or hate the idea, you haven't moved yourself any closer to writing it.

So don't talk about your ideas: *Write them first.*

When you've got enough down on paper for a mentor to peek at, that's the time to open up about your project and get feedback and ideas. Once there's a rough draft.

A good way to know when something is ready for a mentor to look at is if you've done not one, but four solid drafts. This is something that varies widely between people, but hear me out. Obviously, if a method works for you (whether it's one draft, or outlining, or fifteen drafts, or what) that's great. But if you're the kind of writer who has a lot of great ideas but never gets them down for some reason, try this:

Write at least four solid drafts before you show work to others:

1. Write a complete rough draft (rough draft 1).

It's imperative at this initial stage that you force yourself to not rewrite or revise, lest you get endlessly mired in minute edits and revisions to the early pages, while leaving vast or important sections completely unwritten. This is a form of writer's block, and a deceptive one: You feel like you're writing, even though you're not getting anywhere. Even if you know for sure you'll change something, just make a note and keep marching on until the end.

Pro Tip: Many writers find that leaving a chapter (or even a sentence!) unfinished can help jump-start their writing when they come back the next day.

2. Reread and revise that draft (rough draft 2).

Now's where you make those edits and corrections and such that you forced yourself to not make in Rough draft 1.

3. Print the new version out and read that, making handwritten corrections.

4. Copy these corrections back into the document, along with anything else you find (rough draft 3).

5. Read and edit this draft (rough draft 4 and final draft 1).

This final document is your finished first final draft.

At this point, you should have made this work absolutely the best that it can possibly be on your own. If you find out that it's 800 pages, well, maybe you want to keep on editing. Brilliant as you think it may be. But if it's the best you can make it, it's ready for a mentor to see. And maybe to show to some good "target readers" who will give you feedback, support, or advice.

But don't think you're done. Far from it. You will need to edit and revise *this* draft numerous times, maybe even toss it out completely and rewrite from the ground up, to get things right.

My debut novel, *Sunsets of Tulum*, was published after its fortieth "final" draft.

Many people rush to show their work after completing rough draft 1, when it's so raw, unedited, or even just plain bad that they haven't given it a good chance. Even worse, many people send that barely finished draft off to publishers and agents, hoping that someone will see a kernel of value there and decide to "adopt" a new, fledgling writer. That doesn't happen anymore. If it ever did. They're showing their work at its most raw, least polished, least professional.

Don't be that writer. Don't make that mistake.

Take the time to learn the craft, to work through *numerous* drafts, show it to mentors and incorporate their feedback and advice. Then and only then is it time to search for an agent or publisher.

The only way you'll be traditionally published is by chipping away at your manuscript until it is truly as good as you can make it, accepting feedback from mentors and others who can offer you constructive criticism designed to improve the book and its salability, and then submitting to agents a work that's truly top of its class. There are a hundred writers out there, ten of them as good or better than you are. Don't waste that chance with an agent by presenting shoddy work.

And did someone just say agent?

6

Queries and Agents and Publishers, Oh My!

At some point, when your writing has developed and matured, when you've rigorously improved your craft to where it's the best that it can be, and when your mentors feel your manuscript is ready to be submitted, you'll likely want to search for an agent.

Or maybe not.

There are times when an agent really won't help you much, such as if you're a short-story writer, doing articles for newspapers and magazines, or some other short form endevour. Agents usually sign on for long works such as memoirs or novels, though there are exceptions. But if you're not doing long projects, just cross out "agent" in this chapter and put "editor" and send your work out to literary magazines or papers. This chapter was written with the fiction writer in mind; you may find other fields have different needs. Or you may feel you don't want to give the lion's share of your profits to publishers and opt to self-publish from the start. Totally up to you.

Most of you with a longer work, a book, a novel, a memoir, that sort of thing, will need to choose between traditional publishing and self-publishing. Each has its advantages and drawbacks. If you go the traditional route, you *will* need an agent. Publishers simply do not accept over-the-transom submissions anymore, least of all from people just starting out who don't have a starry record of best sellers. Stephen King might be able to cozy up to an editor directly.

The rest of us? No.

Finding an agent

Amateur writers tend to think that getting an agent works like this: You whip out a book and shotgun your submission out to 100 agents the moment you've put down the pen or turned off the computer, and magically, they love it and you get fifty "We want to represent you!"s in a week. They also think that an agent is someone who will "adopt" a writer, coax them through the process of learning to write, put up with foibles and mistakes and personal issues, all because they believe in the wonder of the manuscript in front of them.

If you think that's how it works, that cliché about swampland in Florida for sale may apply.

Agents are in a business, a business that is ever more harsh, ever more cutthroat, with fewer margins for profit and even less for error. If they take on a project that doesn't sell, they've lost money. They do that once, it's a mistake. They do it a bunch, they won't be making the rent on that swanky NYC corner office.

So no matter what lovely kernel of poetic beauty lies inside your lovely error-ridden manuscript, an agent who doesn't see it as something that will sell ASAP won't decide to represent you.

Don't be discouraged. Don't take this personally. Don't rant and rave against a system that's stacked against you. That's just the way it is. Admit it: Even you don't want to waste your time reading someone else's shoddy, terribly written book. Why would any reader? We all have better things to do with our time.

So if your novel isn't really right for representation, the incredible thing is that it's easier now to be published independently than ever. You can still get your darlings out into the world.

Before you submit

Before submitting to a professional, you want to do several things. Assuming you have a stellar, compelling manuscript that's ready for an agent to jump on board, the biggest reason that you'll be rejected is because, just as they'll tell you in the form rejection, the project isn't really right for representation at that particular place. Really, I don't want to be cruel here, but I spent two years working for a literary agent as a slushpile reader, the first defense against the barrage of queries that came in. Nearly all of them were not worthy of the agent's time, nor even mine (and I was a lowly intern). They were poorly written (a few were even on crumpled yellow legal papers with handwritten scrawl!), they were riddled with typos, errors, hastily churned out by people who couldn't tell the difference between "their" and "there" or didn't care enough to reread.

But even when the technical side was on target, when I could read the query without wincing, it was clear that many people simply chose the agency out of a hat. Writers often submit willy-nilly, completely clueless about what kind of work an agent does or doesn't represent. An agent for children's books will get a query about naval history. A naval history agent will get queried about steamy romance. And so on.

So do your homework here. Really put some careful time into figuring out who is a good fit for your manuscript. And if nobody is, don't delude yourself into thinking that just because you claim it's like *The Grapes of Wrath* or *Moby-Dick* the agent will agree there's a resemblance.

There are websites out there that will track queries, help you identify agents, and so on. Yearly directories of agents, publishers, editors, and so on can be purchased or gotten out of your local library. Be diligent about reading exactly what kind of work an agent is looking to represent, and take the time to track down and read what they've recently represented.

Because while an agent really doesn't want to bother with something they don't represent, the flip side is they really *do* want to be shown work that's similar to something they've already seen do well. So if you've got a manuscript right in line with what they handle, you've got far greater chances of their saying yes.

Be honest with yourself and your submission

I see a lot of amateur writers make the mistake of thinking they can stretch the truth. They have an arty manuscript that's a thinly veiled fiction based on their own life, and they write a query letter that sounds like they've written a giant blockbuster. You see the problem there?

If an agent nibbles and requests more, they're going to be disappointed. You've wasted their time (and yours) by being dishonest about the work, the market, its chances of success. Sometimes this is unintentional, as we tend to be enamored with our own writing and sometimes (as with our kids!) see only the wonder and joy. You, first-time writer, may not have the grasp of the market that a twenty-year veteran agent does. But if you're not writing *The Hunt for Red October*, don't market it as that.

Be honest. Honest with yourself. Honest with that future agent. Let the work's quality and care speak for itself, let the agent figure out the value, and thus, you ensure that if someone does want to see more they won't be immediately disappointed.

How to write a great query

What people don't realize about a query letter is that it's not about you, not about your work, not about your background. It's a tool by which an agent (or, more likely, the intern reading that agent's slushpile while taking graduate classes or working at Walmart) can quickly winnow out the dirt from the gold. Writers think the query is their way to introduce themselves, but in reality, this is the first tool an agent will use to toss your work into the trash. A spelling error, rudeness, overconfidence, blathering on and on, snarkiness, careless typos, anything and everything can set that reader against you.

If that sounds harsh, let me put it this way: The query is one lone page, not more than three paragraphs. You're trying to interest a professional, someone who will vouch for you to publishers who are experts in the field and work with you for months, even years, on your behalf. And pay you. You're expecting all that while telling me that you can't take the time and care to make one lone page absolutely perfect?! No. Just no. Your query letter has to be *absolutely* (insert expletive here!) perfect.

If you can't read, edit, and revise that one page until it's flawless, it won't bode well for your being able to read, edit, or revise an entire manuscript under the pressure of tight deadlines and publishing schedules.

What should my query letter say?

This is relatively easy. You want to introduce the work, explain why the agent will want to see it, and offer relevant (emphasis on relevant!) info about yourself that will establish you. Three paragraphs max. Never more than a lone, lots-of-white-space-on-it single page. Here's an example (and on an 8½-by-11-inch page it's got a lot of white space):

Dear So-and-So,

Hi, my name is Ray Bartlett, and I'm hoping you'll consider representing my novel, Dogs Embarrassing Themselves. *I noticed you represented the best selling* Cats Embarrassing Themselves, *and this book is along similar lines, only for dog lovers. I've copied the first five pages as per your submission guidelines into the bottom of this email.*

The novel begins with dogs doing what they do best: ingratiating themselves to their respective humans in comical ways. Tension develops when a new dog, Fido, arrives on the block and can't quite fit in, but a veteran dog, Rover, takes him under his wing and shows him the ropes. There are ups and downs and a lot of barking, but eventually both Fido and Rover have learned some new tricks. It's a heartwarming tale of furry friendship that I know any dog owner will love.

I'm a longtime dog owner myself, and have rescued several dogs over the years. I'm an active participant in my local dog lovers' club. Nearly half the population of the United States has dogs and there's a constant market for dog-affirming stories just like this; there's even a story line that, like Marley & Me, *might be easily adapted into a Hollywood film.*

Best regards, and I look forward to hearing from you.

   Ray Bartlett

I've written place-holder text and the first and second paragraphs don't really match (I'm not working on a book about dogs), but the purpose of these paragraphs remains the same:

1. Paragraph One: Introduce the work in a few brief sentences, and demonstrate you're attentive to the needs of that particular agent (note the line about

"copying the first five pages" — that comes from my going to that agent's submission guidelines and specifically tailoring this query to them). I've also used a current work, ideally within the past five years, as a comparison.

2. Paragraph Two: Explain the book with a quick overview of characters and plot. People often wander around here, not understanding how to quickly and concisely talk about their work. You're not telling your or the characters' life stories. You're honing in on a few key things that, again, will give the agent a glimmer of whether this book is right for them. Summarize, don't paraphrase. And keep it short, short, short.

3. Lastly, for Paragraph Three, talk about yourself but *only if there's anything to talk about*. Don't talk about stuff that isn't relevant, like how you were the chess champion of your hometown at age fifteen or how you won the quilting award (unless the books are about chess or quilting, of course!).

Don't put down that you won the sixth grade poetry contest when you're now a grandma. You want to pull in only relevant info that sets you up as an expert or authority in that topic. Otherwise, just hope the work speaks for itself and the agent enjoys it.

4. No matter how brilliant you think you are, you will shoot yourself in the foot if the query is longer than a page. Keep it simple, Stooopid. One. Short. Page. Don't be cutesy, don't be snarky. Just be respectful, professional, and nice.

Wash, rinse, repeat

Be prepared to do this a lot. Do your research each time. Identify a good match, go to their website and find exactly what they want you to send, and follow that to the letter. Cross every T. Dot every I. If they want the first twenty pages, don't send them twenty-one or nineteen. If they want 1000 words, don't send them 1001. Show them from the start that you are serious, conscientious, and attentive to detail. Get each query perfect. If you'll be expecting them to treat you and your 300-page manuscript with care, giving them a perfect query is the least you can do.

And you may do that thirty, maybe forty times, maybe a hundred, before you find an agent. Note that I am NOT saying "send it out to thirty or forty agents and you'll get accepted." No. Assuming you have an off-the-shelf, ready-to-go, absolutely perfect manuscript, and assuming that you've carefully and diligently targeted your queries to agents who are highly likely to represent your kind of work…EVEN THEN, prepare to try, try again. If you get lucky, an agent will represent you.

You have an agent, now what?

If you get representation, you probably will want to start depending on that agent for your answers from here on in and may not need this book. Give it to some new beginning writer or, heck, buy them their own copy. The agent is your resource now, so you should get full use out of that ten to fifteen percent you're paying them. They will guide you through, hopefully, to publication. Whole books have been written about what an agent can and can't do for you, so I'll keep this brief. Basically, the agent will shop your book around to publishers and try to get you the very best deal possible. It's in their own best interests: They make a percentage off what you make, so a bigger contract for you means more money for them as well.

No agent should request a reading fee. As anywhere, there are unscrupulous agents, and one of the ways hopeful writers can be taken advantage of is by having to pay up front for services. You shouldn't pay an agent to evaluate whether they want to represent you. Contests charge a reading fee to enter. Agents do not.

When to consider other options

If you're not having success attracting an agent, and more importantly, if all you're getting back are form rejections or no replies at all, it's time to go back to the drawing board. Some agents are willing to offer a bit more info about why they didn't accept your work, so pay attention to what they do say if the rejection goes beyond a few-sentence form letter. Some will invite you to submit again if you address certain issues.

But sometimes you won't get any feedback from agents at all. Don't take it personally. Don't wheedle or beg. Don't fire back scathing rancor about how you deserve better. It didn't cost you anything to submit your work; they're under no obligation whatsoever. (Though in truth, even good, well-meaning agents can be frustratingly lax. Nearly all submissions are digital these days, and it takes hardly any time to plop a bunch of email addresses into a BCC field and send out a form rejection. That's the least that writers should expect, but it seems to happen less and less often. You may send your work off and hear absolutely nothing at all.)

If you don't get any response, try going back to your mentors and asking them for advice. Maybe they're able to help you hone in on what your manuscript lacks. Maybe you jumped the gun and it's just not a publishable work yet. Maybe it will never be. It's a hard thing to accept, but you may have to scratch this project and work on your next idea. (I wrote six "throat-clearing" novels before *Sunsets of Tulum* was published. Yep. Six. Not to mention dozens of short stories, articles, and a thesis for a graduate fiction program.)

If your mentors aren't useful, consider getting outside paid help from a service or professional. GrubStreet.org is a nonprofit that has excellent services for hire. There are loads of them, and they are ever changing, so the internet may be your best resource here. Services are also in the classified section of *Poets & Writers* magazine.

Self-publishing

It used to be that if all else failed one would consider vanity publishing, the last resort for the truly narcissistic…and only those rich enough could afford it. Wanna-be "authors" ponied up thousands of dollars to see their book in print, usually shoddily, hastily done; they were often required to purchase hundreds or thousands of copies at a time.

Those times are gone, baby, gone.

Now it's almost the reverse: The narcissistic insist on a traditional publisher, an agent, going that route because they want to prove to the world how awesome they are. The rest, the ones who just want to write and keep moving forward, publish their work on their own in any numbers of ways. Some self-published writers have become millionaires. Even for those who don't break through financially, self-publishing has a respect that it never did before. It's a genuinely viable option and has made the field of publishing far more democratic than ever. Each self-publishing option has pros and cons.

The Internet

The easiest and cheapest way to get your work out into the world is to put it online. You can serialize it into a personal blog, you can offer it as a downloadable PDF, you can upload it to fan fiction sites or places like Scribd that do online lending. I'm not going to go into the myriad ways one can publish online, but it's cheap (or even free!), fast, and easy, and it can be both emotionally and financially rewarding. It's also vast: Your work can be accessed by anyone anywhere in the world with hardly any barriers. Your word processing software probably even has the option to export your file directly to HTML code, making it easy to cut and paste into a website.

Print-on-Demand

On the other side of the self-publishing industry are the print-on-demand (POD) places, such as CreateSpace (now Amazon-owned), IngramSpark, Lulu, and others. These companies allow you to upload cover art and a formatted manuscript, and they will print copies for you as needed. One at a time if you wish. Ten at a time. Hundreds. Whatever you need. They often offer both an electronic version and paperback. Some even offer hardcover. If you're one of those writers who has to have the real book in your real hands, then POD publishing is the way to go.

Hybrid Publishers

Sitting in the middle between traditional publishers and the POD services are what's known as Hybrids: small, indie publishers (sometimes just one person or a small team) that will offer editorial suggestions and some of what you might find at a traditional house, but that use the bigger companies POD services to produce the actual books. They don't have presses of their own.

Publishing by hand

It's feasible today to even publish by hand, using machines that are sort of like "photocopiers" but put out books instead of sheets of paper. The Harvard Book Store has one of these amazing devices, and you can simply walk in with your ready-to-go files and be walking out with your books in a matter of minutes. (Well, maybe hours.) This is great for people who plan to do most of the marketing and selling on their own or through their networks, and don't need a book to be available for worldwide distribution via the online book giants.

Self-Problems in Self-Paradise

The problem with self-publishing is that it's easier than ever for crap to make it into print, stuff that should never have been published but was written by someone hasty, impatient, who didn't know how to write. They just went ahead and published anyway. Without editors, without proofreaders, without even knowing how to write, many writers just run to the press. There's now an explosion of books out there so riddled with errors and issues that no reader would spend ten minutes on them… let alone ten dollars.

So if you're going to self-publish, you have to bring all the oomph that a traditional publisher would to the table all on your own. I can't go into all the details required, but there are numerous books and online guides about self-publishing. Here's a quick checklist of what you'll need to do before you can confidently bring a self-published work to the world:

1. *Write the best damn book you possibly can.*

2. *Hire an independent editor, someone who can be critical, even harsh.*

3. *Have the finished manuscript professionally proofread and copy edited.*

4. *Have the manuscript typeset and formatted for print/ebook.*

5. *Design or purchase a compelling cover.*

6. *Get an ISBN number (this uniquely codes your book for sale and publication) or use a free one from the POD publisher.*

7. *Generate all the book's metadata (the info about the book for bookstore and library needs).*

8. *Navigate the POD websites and select one.*

9. *Print, market, and distribute your book.*

Another problem is that it's often a challenge to make money if you're self-publishing. While profit often isn't the main reason behind our noble writing dreams, it's not a bad thing to be able to make it pay for itself or buy your mentor a cup of coffee, or heck, pay the rent. Making a buck on your years of effort feels great. I recommend it highly.

But to make money, you really have to sell a lot of books.

To give you a sense of scale, most self-published books sell fewer than 200 copies.

Generally I've avoided using dollar figures here, since it's easy to date an edition by tying it to actual dollars. But as a snapshot, in 2020 (at the time of this printing!), to produce a book you may pay $800 to $1000 for a professional proofreader, $500 for a cover designer, and $500 for additional editing. ISBN numbers (you'll need more than one if you'll have several versions of the book) cost about $300 or more. Some POD sites require a fee to use their services.

So expect to pay between $1500 and $3000 (again, in current, year 2020 prices) to put out a decent, professionally proofed and edited book.

Now consider that you can price a paperback at maybe $10, maybe $15. An e-book might price between 99 cents and $5. Of which you will receive some, not all, of the profit. Your cost of producing a paperback may be about $3 to $5. So you may make about $5 per book if the price is $10.

That is much more than the fractional amount you'd make if the book were with a traditional publisher. But to pay for itself, your paperback will need to sell $3000 divided by $5 per book equals a whopping 600 copies.

That's just to break even. You have to sell 601 copies before you can even buy a sandwich.

A traditional publishing house may offer you something around $8000 to $10,000, for comparison, for a basic advance on a first-time novel. And they'll handle all the other stuff on their own. All you do is pay the agent their percentage, pocket the rest of that tasty advance, and start working on your new book. While there are times when a book may tank and you, the author, have to return that advance, most of the time the publisher is willing to absorb that financial hit. They'll also reap the lion's share of the rewards if the book does well. An author who is extremely diligent and hard-working might produce a book a year. Often it's years between books, depending on the author and the genre of fiction. So making $8000 to $10,000 a year is not going to pay for too many New York City condos. If a traditionally published book sells 2000 copies or more in the first six months, it's done "well." Ten thousand or more will bring it to the best seller's lists, but you still may make only a dollar or less per book. So to make a full-time living you'll need to be pushing out best sellers year after year that sell millions of copies and stay on the charts for months.

In short, either way you cut it, don't be writing for the money. Write because you love it, because you're bringing something vital to the world, because you have something amazing to say ... not because you think it's going to earn you a swanky living. There are lucky exceptions, but most writers are not in the top one percent unless they were already born there.

And back to the self-published author: You have to sell 600 copies *just to break even*. So if you're writing because you think it's a quick way to fame and fortune, you should probably opt for life in an internet startup instead. Or win the lottery. Few writers ever become household names or make enough money to turn writing into their full-time day jobs.

Each route has advantages and disadvantages. If you're planning on making a living as a writer anytime soon, you will likely want to focus on writing manuscripts that attract agents and traditional publishers, probably in the main genres like science fiction or mystery or romance. If you merely want to have a tangible product for friends and family, self-publishing through POD gives you a lot of choice and control. And it's certainly true that some self-published writers are able to sell far more copies than the minimum needed to break even. But to do that, self-published authors will need to put far more energy into the marketing of themselves and their work than someone traditionally published.

If you've got deep pockets, you can hire a publicist. They'll handle a lot of the marketing and such for you, but the trick is you really have to have this all set up at least six months in advance. Otherwise there's just not enough time for them to make arrangements and get things going for you. A major-league publicist might add another $6000 to the price tag of your indie-published book. Meaning you'd need to sell about 1800 copies before you can get that sandwich.

Going the indie route, however, can work financially if you churn out books, and many feel the best avenue is to skip print completely and focus on e-books only. There's far less formatting required, and less investment, and if you realize your name's misspelled on the title page, it can be fixed faster and more cheaply than if you've typeset for print.

Whether you opt for a traditional publishing route or you self-publish will be specific to your individual needs and dreams. Either way, knowing the ins and outs, the goods and bads, the pros and cons, will help you make the decision that's right for you.

7

Persist or Perish

Much of your writing success will depend on how well you can just keep on keeping on. There's a lot of waiting that happens, a lot of developing, a lot of gestation. And frustration, self-doubt, insecurity. All those things wrap into a big ball of uncertainty that sidelines many would-be writers. It's just too hard to keep pushing forward when you don't know if your work is any good (Get a mentor!) or whether you'll be able to do it (Set those goals!) or whether you'll ever break through (Make luck happen!). Hopefully the previous chapters have given you good tools for setting this journey in motion, but for most of us, being a writer isn't going to happen overnight. You have to persist. You have to be in this for the long haul.

While I always wanted to be a writer, for most of high school and college, I thought I could easily enjoy a career as an actor or an artist as well. The question was which path to follow. I chose art as my major. My college didn't have a creative writing program, and I was a bit conceited about my writing ability back then, didn't see much use for English classes – who needed them? I was already so good, I didn't need to learn. (Note the heavy sarcasm.)

Despite being a small, liberal arts school, my college offered a novella contest each fall, to which I avidly submitted a fifty-page masterpiece. The first prize was $700, with a fancy dinner, and there were not only second- and third-place winners, but three honorable mentions.

For four years I entered. And four years I failed to receive even a measly honorable mention. Clearly my masterpieces weren't as masterful as I imagined. But it was a bit discouraging to do the math and realize there could not have been many entries in such a small school. Knowing I was number seven out of seven stung.

Then, in my senior year, a bit of chaos happened: My girlfriend of two years broke up with me, a tragicomedy that left me wondering if my creative artistic life was really worth pursuing after all. In a bizarre, self-flagellatory decision that would send even medieval monks into rapture, I dropped my art studio major and switched to poly-econ, the course of study that included not only my beloved, but her new beau as well. To fulfill the needs of the major I would have to take an extra summer and one more semester of college, graduating not in four years, but in four and a half.

This gave me one last chance to enter that damn novella contest.

And to my surprise and genuine shock, that final autumn I was the first-prize winner. That one lone short story, "Lilac and Me," set in a small Southwestern town, went on to win an honorable mention in another contest, and then an additional creative writing award. In all, I won so much prize money from that one story that I was able to quit my work-study job that final year.

More importantly, that's when I made the decision that I would pursue neither art nor acting as a career; I would be a writer.

I was lucky to win, for sure. I was even lucky that my girlfriend broke up with me. But had I not *persisted*, had I not dutifully submitted novellas in hopes of winning that prize, I wouldn't have ever won. Nobody other than myself was pushing me to write or submit. I was busy with school, I had my breakup and social stuff happening. *Not writing* would have been far easier, especially since I didn't expect to win anyway. Yet I kept on going. Had I not, I might never have had that chance and my life might be radically different from what it is today. I was lucky, sure. But I also made luck happen, just as you will if you stick with it.

So plan on persisting with this writer thing. It's your only way to eventually make it happen.

Another anecdote, again pulled directly from my own life, about the value of persistence:

After college, I was lucky enough to spend two years in Japan teaching English in the far south of Japan. It was a magical experience, rife with wonder and anecdotes so rich that I felt compelled to put it all into a memoir. As soon as I returned home to the United States, I spent about ten months writing up what would become the book *In the Sunlight of Sakurajima: My Two Years Living in Southern Japan.*

I tried unsuccessfully to interest an agent or publisher. Among the places I tried, I queried Lonely Planet, which at the time was the largest privately owned travel publisher in the world. It had become famous for their country guidebooks, big thick tomes that travelers all over the world affectionately called their "bibles" as they meandered the globe. For a certain generation, if you were traveling anywhere, you went out and got a Lonely Planet for the destination.

In addition to its country guides, however, it also published a variety of other books, including Alex Kerr's *Lost Japan*, a well-known nonfiction title about modern Japan. I felt my memoir fit nicely in that vein and sent off a query letter full of hope and optimism.

They rejected me.

It was a typical email form rejection. The worst kind. I probably still have it somewhere in my files, but the gist was the usual two sentences. Something like, "Thank you for your interest, but this doesn't suit our current editorial needs. We wish you luck placing it elsewhere."

Disappointed but undaunted, I thanked them with a short reply and added that if they ever needed someone to work on their country guide to Japan, I was fluent in Japanese (at the time, a bit of a stretch), had lived there, and knew the country well.

The reply was even more brief, and I could almost hear the frost:

"We will put you on the list."

I translated that immediately to "Please stop pestering us, as we never want to hear from you again."

So that was that. I queried numerous other publishers about my book and eventually set it aside for nearly twenty years before eventually opting to self-publish it. (To this day, it still sells a few copies monthly and brings me a weensy royalty payment from Amazon. I'm content.)

However, back to the story: A few years went by.

And then one day, just as I was about to "Delete All" from my spam folder, on an email address I rarely ever used, I noticed a subject line that did not seem to be for prescription meds or discount sneakers or sunglasses.

It was from Lonely Planet.

"We have had an opening in our guidebook to Japan and are wondering if you are still available to work for us."

It came at a really hard time for me personally. A number of things had been happening in my life, including the passing of my grandfather, a mentor and friend, and someone who'd always supported me and admired my passionate pursuit of being a writer. This little bit of incredible luck couldn't have happened at a darker time, and I wrote back immediately. A few days later they sent me the "test" part of the application.

Writing is such a strange thing, because you don't need to have a degree or document or even a resume sometimes. You just have to write well. By that time, I'd graduated from Boston University's fiction program. I'd had numerous pieces published in travel magazines and newspapers. I wasn't doing enough to make this my living (I was teaching college at the time), but I finally felt like there was momentum. That same momentum I talked about back in Chapter Two.

The test involved writing an entire chapter of a Lonely Planet guidebook, all of it, from soup to nuts. The intro, the hotels, the restaurants, the sights, even the maps. You got to choose where you wrote, but it had to be as if you were going to put it into a LP guide to that place.

"I've got this," I thought, confident that my experience working for other magazines and doing travel pieces would carry me through with flying colors. But what worried me was the maps. I'd never done any cartography before. Many of my articles included my photos, but that was easy: Just snap a picture and you're done. This was a different animal completely. I had to create original maps, have sources, have everything to scale.

So I went at it, working up a chapter of golden prose and spending days painstakingly creating maps. I sent it off with trepidation, and sure enough, within a week, I got the news:

"We're sorry to say that this submission didn't meet our standards. The maps were excellent, but the writing just wasn't up to par."

They liked the maps.

It was as if they'd squirted lime juice into the wound.

My grandfather passed away, and for a few days I felt like things couldn't get any lower. (Remember, I adhere to the maxim that one shouldn't talk about writing, so I had not mentioned this to anyone, not even my family, not even to my wife!) To be so close and yet have this chance vanish. I'm not sure what I did specifically, but there was likely some alcohol involved.

And then I decided to do what a writer should never do.

I asked for another chance.

If there's one thing editors and agents hate, it's being pestered. If they've offered you a clear window of time and made a decision, they do *not* want to have to revisit you again and again. If a story gets rejected, you dust yourself off and submit to somewhere else.

You don't go groveling back to the same editor and wheedle that they need to give you another chance.

But this was the exception. I really had nothing to lose.

In my most respectful, polite wording, I asked if they'd consider giving me another chance. There's a part of me that still wonders if this could have been partly a ploy on their part, to test how well I take rejection, to see whether I'd explode in fury or whimper away with my tail between my legs. But regardless of what their motives were, mine were clear: I wanted to get that job.

So I persisted. I asked, nicely, for another shot.

And they said yes.

I felt like I had just won a million-dollar lottery.

And this time, I didn't change the maps at all. But I got out every Lonely Planet title I could from the library and hoovered up the style, the tone, the humor. (Think Rocky Balboa and the staircase, music of champions in the background.) I put every ounce of energy into matching that iconic voice, into making my chapter fit perfectly into their existing works. I was like a painter creating fake Monets, I was so focused on copying the prose.

And that second time, it passed muster. They were probably as desperate for a writer as I was to write for them, who knows, but a month later I was writing for *Lonely Planet* in Hokkaidō, Japan. My life took a right turn, and that to this day is the biggest break I've ever had. Shortly after that I stopped teaching altogether and was, for the first time, writing full time.

All because of one thing: *I didn't give up.*

It wasn't easy.

And a vast world of other choices had to be made, choices that would affect my life, my family, my future.

But if I'd chosen to accept that initial rejection of my manuscript and hadn't offered myself as a writer, or if I'd chosen to accept their rejection of my first test, I wouldn't be writing this book today. I like to think some other luck would have happened, because I feel strongly that we make our own luck. But my life would be very, very different.

So persist, persist, persist.

Say it the way you would a mantra.

Because it is. If you persist, you'll make luck happen. You'll be there at just the right time. You'll have that big break. But only if you persist at it.

Ensure financial stability

Unfortunately, short of being a trust-fund baby, marrying rich, or being a lottery winner, most of us have to still earn a living while we work our way slowly into having writing be our full-time career. And a lot of persisting is about making the ends meet in the meantime.

Everyone has different thresholds, different standards of living below which they can't allow themselves to fall. You can't be criticized for doing something 9 to 5 that puts food on the table. And the good news is that if you've made writing an integral part of your day, if you've set your short-, medium-, and long-term goals, if you've found mentors, if you're pushing yourself to complete work rather than circle around in eddies, guess what? You can have a full-time job and still make your creative dreams come true if you've got those goals set and you're diligent about quality and quantity of your craft.

Of all the events in my life, none was bigger than the news that I was going to be a dad. For the first time in my life, I had to think about someone other than myself, and despite being a full-time writer, I jumped into job hunting for a "real" job. A part of me worried that this would end my writing career, that I'd end up too mired in parenting to make any writing happen. That the needs of a day job would leave me so exhausted by the end of the day that I'd have no energy to write.

And how did things turn out?

The opposite happened.

I was already so attuned to writing that I found it relaxing to get to the computer for ten or fifteen minutes or an hour. Whenever I could, there I'd be, typing away at this project or another. I published my debut novel, *Sunsets of Tulum*. I wrote another (*Celadon*). I continued to work on best-selling travel guides to Mexico, Japan, and other parts of the world. Five years slipped by and I'd been actively writing the entire time. When my day job let me go, I jumped right back to writing full time without missing a beat. My daughter, no surprise, says she wants to be a writer when she grows up. I have vivid memories of her asleep in my lap at three in the morning as I kept her company (and let my wife get some shut-eye!)...all while never losing touch with my writing goals.

Put another way: Writing will be your chance to put your money where your mouth is. Into every life come issues, problems, hurdles, complications. You have a choice to make. Either keep on writing, through thick or thin, or press pause. I'd argue that the latter is dangerous, but for some, this may be just what you need to do. You can always unpause down the road.

Luck won't come if you're not allowing it to. Don't let anything become an excuse for not writing. I hear a lot of people make excuses for why they've let a year, two, three, a decade slip by without writing.

Don't be one of those people.

A writer will still write no matter what else is going on.

8

When Writer's Block Rears its Ugly Head

Writer's block happens even to the best of us, and oddly, you can be writing like a mad dervish and still be just as blocked as if you were not writing at all.

Most people think of writer's block as something that just – like it sounds – prevents you from putting words to the page. You sit down at the computer, open up your document, and ... nothing.

But far more insidious is the writer's block that comes in the form of you madly, even enthusiastically, typing away at this or that, not realizing that instead of moving somewhere, you're actually caught in an eddy, going in circles, round and round. It seems like productivity, but it's not. In a way, it's even worse than staring at a blank page, because you don't realize you're blocked.

I already mentioned how this can happen when you are writing that first, initial rough draft: You sit down and, for whatever reason, you don't go to where you left off at the end of the document, but scroll back to the beginning. In moments you've spotted an error, realized a word needs tweaking, found a bit of punctuation you'd like to change, and you're off: an hour or two passes, and (here's why this is an eddy!) you're not a sentence closer to finishing the book or moving further in that scene you've been stuck on and stopped writing a week ago.

Some people will do this endlessly, feeling they have nothing to lose by pushing words around a little bit before delving into the task at hand. It feels like writing, really, it does. But it isn't.

That little bit of editing consumes your time, your energy, and your creativity. Before you know it, it's time for lunch, then you have to walk the dog or grab the kids, and your whole day is done.

Without a new word having been written.

There's also writer's block that comes as one nears the finish line. You are literally at the end of this marathon, you've got most of the work done, you know where you have to go with it …

… and yet you somehow just lose the interest and oomph to keep going. You sit down and feel blah, nothing sounds good, nothing works anymore. You're so close, and yet so far.

Both of these situations come from an inner failure to confront the task at hand. In the first case, where you endlessly revise the beginning, you're avoiding addressing some trickier element that got you off track. Maybe you realized a character isn't as strong as you thought. Or a scene you expected to be thrilling isn't working out. Any number of things.

In the latter, you're struggling because you're nearly done with a project that's been a part of you for months, years, even decades. You've had it inside you all this time and now, terrifyingly, it's about to be born. It won't be that book you know you can write if you try anymore. You're about to say goodbye to a close friend forever. And you don't want to.

This "friendship" you've had, this love, this part of yourself, is going to fly away into other readers' arms and be their baby, not yours anymore. That's scary and unnerving. You want it to be perfect, and yet you're seeing now that it won't be. After all this time and effort, it's not good enough. The real book isn't quite matching up with your glowing expectations.

The solution to both of these is to give yourself the luxury to be bad.

All those times I said you want to be your own worst critic? Well, here's where you get to pat yourself on the back and look in the mirror and take a deep breath: You can do this. Just get the damn thing done.

You can do this. Push through. And you can come back to it later if you need to. Just get that draft done.

If you're stuck on a particular scene or dialogue, one easy solution, something I do all the time, is to write a little note (I don't even bother with the Comments feature of my word processing program, I just do it with "*****" or "XYZ – write this later" or something) and forge ahead. I've skipped the problem completely. And by letting myself come back to it, solve it later, I'm suddenly free to focus on scenes where I do have some enthusiasm or energy. And nine times out of ten, by the time I'm done, I've had enough time to know exactly what I want to do with that "problem." It's solved itself.

Likewise, as you're nearing the climactic end of your novel, there's a sense that it has to be incredible, powerful, earth-shattering right now. But guess what? You can write a really bland, even boring ending (not that we want to aim for that!) and come back to it after getting feedback from friends or mentors. You can even tell them, "I'm really unhappy with the final few scenes; would love your suggestions."

And readers love being able to offer some helpful insights. Making their participation important heightens their involvement. Friends feel necessary and helpful. So whether you just jot a note to return or write it poorly (again, knowing you'll return and polish it to a shine!), you've freed yourself to keep moving, which is absolutely vital in that first rough draft. Just get through it, get the damn thing done.

And sometimes taking a break, a walk, a short trip, getting a house task done, something non-writing can free your mind a bit until that unexpected eureka moment comes.

What about writer's block that comes later, after the first draft is done?

Yeah. There's that. You've written your rough draft, you've gotten feedback from mentors, you know what you're going to do. And suddenly the project feels like it's a big fat puddle of molasses around your feet. Every step you try to take is agonizingly slow.

The bad news is that you're into the part of the writing process that actually really *is* agonizingly slow.

The revising. Some writers love this. Others hate it worse than having dental work done.

Endless hours of revising. You will know how Prometheus felt having his liver eaten by an eagle every day. The task of revision and editing.

None of that is nearly as exciting or as rewarding as that first magical drafting was. This feels like you're slogging because, yep, you actually are.

The good news is that this isn't really writer's block. It's just that you're a craftsman and you have to produce a product that's been polished to a shine so bright you can shave in its reflection. Here's where many writers just get impatient. They want to be done, so they convince themselves they *are* done, when they're actually far from it. So just keep going. You'll get there.

I've talked about two types of writer's block that are very common, but there are plenty of others as well.

The "What should I write next?" can happen to writers who have mainly put their eggs into the basket of a lone, often very personal, work. In those cases, you may need to choose between digging deeper into that same material or veering off into a different direction and trying something new. Give yourself time. Try catching up on some reading. Take a trip somewhere. Chances are, just as when you're trying really hard to remember something and it keeps eluding you, so too the spark of inspiration won't catch until you're least expecting it.

But there are other ways to tackle it too: brainstorming to exercises to journaling, these and many other tools exist for helping you break through. Many writing books go into great detail about how to start the ideas flowing, so I've focused more on the causes and solutions here.

Oh, one other tip:

Make writer's block work for you.

I'm not just writing about all these things. I've experienced them myself, many times, and am sharing what's worked well for me. Your mileage may differ.

But I find that I'm often blocked in one project, procrastinating, being lazy, whatever … and yet suddenly I'm gung-ho excited to work on a different project.

And that's exactly what I'll do.

If I'm really stuck, wheels spinning, down to the axles stuck, and another idea is bouncing around in my head, I'll use that energy and go with that for a while. For me, that's helped to ensure that I'm productive, that I don't get bogged down, and that when ideas come and I have the zeal to work on them, I take advantage of that.

So if you're nine-tenths of the way done with your Harry Hamster Heads to Hollywood novel, and suddenly you get an idea for a mystery where talking cars solve crimes, don't feel you have to push those muses off your shoulder until the hamster's hit Hollywood Boulevard.

Chances are, you'll work on the cars project for a bit and by the time that stalls, maybe you'll be pining to polish up that last bit of Harry.

The bottom line is that I want you to experiment with ending your writer's block with *other writing*. Don't procrastinate writing your novel by cleaning the kitchen or playing a video game or mowing the lawn. At least for that hour a day, make your time to write count. Brainstorm, work on a new project, push forward on an established one, but keep on writing. My kitchen is an unmitigated disaster zone, my lawn looks like the house has been abandoned, and the last video game I was good at was in college. But I always have writing projects simmering away, working on this or that as I see the need to. (Okay, for the record, I do sometimes clean the kitchen.)

9

Re-evaluate

As wonderful and appropriate as your goal lists may be, they will not necessarily be the same at age fifteen as they are when you're fifty. Your writing interests, needs, and dreams may shift over time, and it's perfectly acceptable to revisit your goal list if it no longer is going to move you where you want to be.

I remember my short-, medium-, and long-term goals quite well when I was in college:

- Short: *Get published.* (Just about anywhere!)

- Medium: *Get paid for my writing.*

- Long: *Win the Nobel Prize in Literature.*

That set of goals propelled me through the short-term process of dutifully sending out queries to agents, publications, and magazines. It also shifted my writing away from genre fiction and into literary writing. In pursuit of that medium-term goal I began focusing on longer works, novels, rather than continuing with short stories (which I still love).

Fast forward a few decades and my goals are substantially different. I'm a working, full-time writer. I've been able to have requests coming in to me for work rather than having to send out queries to the slushpile. I've got different needs, and a new set of goals is entirely valid. Note these are more demanding than what I had set for myself twenty years ago. I'm not using a process goal now because my process is deeply ingrained. I don't need to set a goal of "writing daily" because that's my default place to be. A lot of other things may not happen today, but I will actually write.

So the goals now are:

- Short: *Complete the first draft of a mystery series.*
- Medium: *Have a successful best-selling novel.*
- Long: *Migrate from travel writing to fiction as my main income source.*

Don't feel like you have to stick to something just…because that's what you thought twenty years ago. These are your goals, so if they're not working for you anymore, shift things around. Adjust and adapt and grow and change. It's all good.

Adjust your lifestyle

Continuing that vein, being a full-time writer for many of us means downsizing your financial dreams. I don't want to get depressing, but writing is probably not going to buy you a chrome-plated Rolls

Royce anytime soon. It may not even pay the bills very well. The average advance for a traditionally published novel is around $8000, and if a writer is *lucky* and extremely diligent, he or she will write a novel a year. $8000 per year. Yes, royalties may turn out to be golden for you, but they may not. It's rare, but writers sometimes have to pay publishers back if the book sells poorly. A new "advance free" publishing option puts even more of the onus on the writers: Some publishers won't even offer an advance. They're happy to take credit (and the cash!) for the project if it sells, but your author pay is entirely on the royalty.

So being a writer, especially a freelance writer, a full-time writer, means adjusting yourself (and your family, if you have one!) to that economic reality.

Adjust your expectations

With that reality comes an adjustment of expectations. You may find that your skills as a writer are most lucrative when you're writing copy for marketing brochures. Copywriting and editing are highly in demand, and it may be that those offer you the financial freedom that your literature never did. As much as you may have expected to live like Richard Castle in a luxurious New York City penthouse (ideally solving crimes with a beautiful detective and having a perfect life!), real writers may struggle to make ends meet, often for years, sometimes for their entire lives. Expecting to waltz into best-sellerdom is unrealistic at best and can even genuinely harm your chances long term by making you think it will all come easily. You can do this. Really. You can. Nothing in this book is rocket science.

But it takes patience and a lot of hard work. You will fight for it, work for it, and make sacrifices to see that dream come true. Your family and friends will have to accept and adjust and adapt. It can be lonely locking yourself in a room all the time. Especially if you're unsure whether this is even the right thing for you to begin with. (Remember, I was maybe going to be an artist or an actor for a while.)

10

Managing Success

If you stick with it, if you make luck happen, there's a point where you may realize that you've achieved success. Maybe your long-term goal is still waiting for you, giving you something to look forward to in the future, but you've published your first, your second, your third book, you've turned writing into a career rather than a hobby you do in your spare time…Now what?

One challenge of writing is that the definition of success changes throughout your career.

Success when you're starting out means getting noticed, getting published, getting that first incredible check, and that validation of your writing. Knowing that it's so darn good that someone is actually willing to pay you for it. Wow.

But a few years down the road, you're regularly publishing and getting paid for it…so success now means you get something big enough to pay the bills. Or to put some money aside. You want to write a best seller. Or sell movie rights.

Then that happens. And success then means making sure that your next book can *also* stay on the best seller charts.

And so on.

My point in providing all these examples is to underline how vital it is that you manage your success. You won't ever be able to fold your arms behind your head, put your feet up on the desk, and say, "I'm there." Each peak you summit will show you a new mountain you need to climb.

Avoiding pitfalls

Unfortunately, there are a number of big things you can do to put a hole into the boat that's your writing career. I can't list them all and hopefully none that I do list will happen to you. Some will seem like basic things and, of course, they apply whether you're a writer or not. But still, you'd be surprised how many people make it big and start to overlook things.

Avoid scandals

While scandal seems to work just fine for Hollywood folks and those in the music biz, it works less well for writers. Getting embroiled in criminal activities, fraud, human trafficking or prostitution, all those things, can bring a speedy end to a writer's budding career. You may not feel like people are looking up to you, but they are, and engaging in crime or getting caught up in scandals shatters that in a way you may not be able to recover from. It also gets in your mental way, or (if you've got court dates to deal with) even physically prevents you from writing. You are focusing your mind on the issue, not on your next book. Be good to people and to yourself.

Avoid time wasters

It's easy as you struggle with trying to make writing happen to get sidetracked into other time-wasting pursuits. The biggest is drugs, alcohol, or other addictions. There's nothing inherently wrong with them. I'm not trying to preach. The list of writers with known addictions runs from Kerouac to Hemingway (and many in between!), to the point that it's easy to say "But they've been amazing writers and been addicted to (fill in the blank), why can't I?"

I promise you, addiction will end up wasting your valuable writing time and pinching your finances. Don't be one of those people who thinks you'll be the next Hunter S. Thompson. The time when people wanted to read Gonzo journalism was decades ago. Being high may seem like it enhances creativity; with very few exceptions, it doesn't. And I've known far too many people who've let drugs control their lives – or end them – to suggest that being cavalier with recreational drugs will help a writing career. Writing's hard enough as it is. Don't make it harder.

Don't anger your readers

Many of us have heard about a writer making off-color comments, sexual or racist or otherwise, and really, the world has very little tolerance these days for that kind of thing. It's very easy to have a flippant comment come out on social media that is interpreted wrongly and blows up into a huge mountain of hurt, damaging your bottom line and leaving otherwise loving readers with the taste of bile in their mouth. Just because you have a platform, hundreds of thousands of readers, doesn't mean you are above them or above being a decent human being. Again: Be good to people and to yourself.

Don't anger your publishers

Sometimes conflicts occur between you and the people who've given you your bread and butter: your publishers. Ego, money, personality conflicts, these can all ignite into a spat that sends you searching for other people to work with. But be careful: New York is a very small town, and angering a publisher or developing a reputation as someone who is difficult to work with can leave you with very few options down the road. Don't be a diva.

Be appreciative and remember how lucky you are.

A writer usually has a bit more privacy than a movie star, in that fewer people will gush and coo over you in a restaurant as you're trying to sip your soup, but it will happen. It's often hard to realize that this annoying person pestering you for an autograph and interrupting your romantic dinner for two is in fact someone who has *paid* you, giving you, obliquely, the means to buy that fancy meal. This person may have halitosis so bad it's withering your face like a prune, but they've got feelings too, and being kind, appreciative, and welcoming will never hurt.

Don't go broke.

Financial ruin is a good way to be a writer who is never heard from again, and writers often feel like once they've had a big break or started to make it, that the gravy train is running and will never dry up again.

Wrong.

Just like anyone else working a 9-to-5, you need to treat your earnings with a keen eye for preparing for the future. Save ten percent of every paycheck. Keep in mind much of your writing will not have taxes taken out, so that can be a huge hit each April. Add to those IRAs. Invest for growth and for stability, reshaping your portfolio as the decades pass to ensure you have the money you need. It's boring to think about money, but it's what gives you the freedom to continue doing what you love.

Don't forget to grow your network

This is a simple one, but it goes beyond having a bunch of followers on Instagram. Be constantly on the lookout for people who will make a difference in your writing career. It could be someone you meet at work or at the gym who has an interest in writing, maybe they'll be a good future reader of your work. Have a web page, be sure to get people to sign up on email. If there are writing-related events in your area, start attending.

And as you become recognized, give back to the community. You're not an island, and a writer who alienates and irritates their community and readership will sell fewer books, have fewer attendees at conferences or signings, and so on.

Yes, there are a few renowned divas who break this mold, but don't be a diva. The world has enough divas already. Be someone whom other aspiring writers appreciate and look up to. And never think any reader is beneath you or not worth your time.

Stay abreast of changes

Who knows what the future holds…and that's exactly the point. Thirty years ago nobody in publishing had a clue that the internet would reshape the publishing landscape so dramatically. Social media has made it easier than ever to be in touch with your community, though that's come at the cost of it being harder to close the door and just write. There are probably people who still write, as Steinbeck did, with a pencil on a yellow legal pad, but they're few and far between and missing out on the incredible tool known as the word processor. There will always be tools out there, useful ways to save time as you write, and you'll want to keep up with these so you don't slip too far behind your peers.

Remember the little people

Going along with the "don't be a diva" I mentioned earlier, no matter how big a writing rock star you manage to become, remember that all around you are people who helped you ascend to that position. Your family, your friends, your teachers, your community. Even if people didn't help you directly, by reading your work, for example, they've contributed in some small way. Be generous and kind and give back when you can, either by volunteering in a local writing group, donating to the organizations that you feel are worthy of support, or other such ways to pay it back and forward. Support other writers where possible, even budding ones in the beginning of their careers. You may find that some of these "lowly" writers become lions and tigers in their own right down the road.

All of these elements will aid you in being there, in just the right place and at just the right time, when luck happens.

With a bit of planning and caution, you can continue your career and reap its benefits for years to come.

Epilogue

Thank you for reading this book, and I hope it has helped you feel there's a path for you to follow, and for you to create your own where there isn't one. These are the tips and tricks I've used, and much of what I teach in my workshops and classes. But if you find that some element is not quite right for you, don't worry: You can certainly cherry-pick exactly the bits and pieces you think make sense and go your own way when our paths differ.

If you have time, I'd greatly appreciate a review on Amazon and Goodreads, and if you have questions, I'm always interested in hearing from readers. The contact info follows on a separate page.

Very best with your creative road, do good work, and be healthy.

— Ray Bartlett

About the Author

Ray Bartlett has written dozens of best-selling travel guidebooks for Lonely Planet, Insight Guides, Moon Handbooks, and other top industry publishers. He is the author of the novels *Sunsets of Tulum* (2015) and *Celadon* (2020) and the memoir *In the Sunlight of Sakurajima* (2015), and he has been featured in numerous magazines, journals, and newspapers worldwide. He also offers manuscript consulting and mentoring services. Contact him via his website (www.kaisora.com) for more info.

When not on the road, Ray enjoys surfing, dancing Argentine tango, cooking, and playing saxophone.

Contact Info

Email: info@kaisora.com

Web: www.kaisora.com

Twitter/Instagram @kaisoradotcom

Facebook: RayBartlettAuthor

YouTube: RayGoesTo

Sign up for Ray's newsletter here:

http://eepurl.com/bVJ4Cz

www.ingramcontent.com/pod-product-compliance
Lightning Source LLC
Chambersburg PA
CBHW052210090526
44584CB00016BA/2061